DISNEY'S
WINNIE the POOH'S
Valentine

by Bruce Talkington
illustrated by John Kurtz

Disney PRESS

NEW YORK

To my wife, Susi,

the BEST valentine I've ever gotten!
—B.T.

Copyright © 1995 by Disney Press.
All rights reserved.
No part of this book may be used or reproduced
in any manner whatsoever without written permission from the publisher.
Printed in the United States of America.
For information address Disney Press,
114 Fifth Avenue, New York, New York 10011.
Based on the Pooh stories by A. A. Milne (copyright The Pooh Properties Trust).

Library of Congress Catalog Card Number: 94-70525
ISBN: 0-7868-3017-4
FIRST EDITION
3 5 7 9 10 8 6 4 2

It was easy to see what day it was in the Hundred-Acre Wood. Birds cuddled in pairs on drooping limbs and were loudly chirping duets. Friendly breezes tickled the leaves of trees until they fluttered with laughter. Saplings shyly touched and, bending close, exchanged sweet secrets in restless whispers. It always seemed, on Valentine's Day, that things were more tightly wrapped around each other than usual, as if Mother and Father Nature were taking advantage of the day to share an extra-large hug.

At Winnie the Pooh's house, things were taking on a decidedly "heartfelt" appearance, mostly because Pooh had just finished tacking up his "felt hearts" (bright red, of course) in all the most *strategic* places. *Strategic,* Owl had once explained, meant the places where things were sure to be in the way and, therefore, attract the most attention. At least, that's how Pooh remembered Owl explaining it, which, as far as he was concerned, made it as true as if Owl had actually said it just that way...which he hadn't.

Pooh's happy contemplation of his handiwork was suddenly interrupted by a quiet voice saying "Pooh Bear" in a most polite tone.

Startled, Pooh turned so quickly he bumped his nose on a felt heart tacked to the back of a very *hard* door.

"Oh bother!" sniffed Pooh as he noticed Roo standing anxiously in the middle of his parlor floor. "Why, hello, little Roo!" he exclaimed, almost forgetting his sore nose in the delight of seeing his friend.

"Hello, Pooh," responded Roo. "Is that felt?" he asked, pointing to the heart.

Pooh cautiously rubbed his nose. "Oh, I felt it, all right," he assured Roo woefully.

"No," said Roo, "is that *heart* felt?"

"Oh!" said Pooh, not really understanding the question, so not feeling the least bit guilty at responding with an answer he found equally confusing: "No, I don't think the heart felt it at all."

Roo smiled brightly at the bear of very little brain and knew that it was time to talk about something else. "Would you mind terribly," he asked politely, "if we talk about something besides your felt hearts?"

"That would be wonderful," breathed Pooh in relief. "What did you have in mind?"

"I want to give a valentine to my mom," Roo whispered, "but I don't know how."

"Neither do I!" laughed Pooh, who was always delighted to agree with someone about something. But his laughter ceased as soon as he saw the look on little Roo's face.

"Then what'll I do?" piped Roo, feeling a distress so profound he could hardly keep his eyes from filling with tears.

"What *we* will do," said Pooh, taking Roo's hand in his own, "is find out!"

In no time at all, Pooh and Roo had gathered together all their best friends—Piglet, Tigger, Rabbit, Gopher, and, of course, Eeyore—and put Roo's question to them.

"Well," suggested Piglet in a very small voice, "the most important thing about a valentine you give to someone is that it says 'I love you.'"

"Yeah!" agreed Tigger, bouncing around Pooh's parlor in excitement. "An' it's got to say it in bright colors!"

"Impressive!" whistled Gopher. "It's got to be impressive 'cause sayin' 'I love you' is a pretty impressive proposition!" He ended with an impressive snap of his fingers.

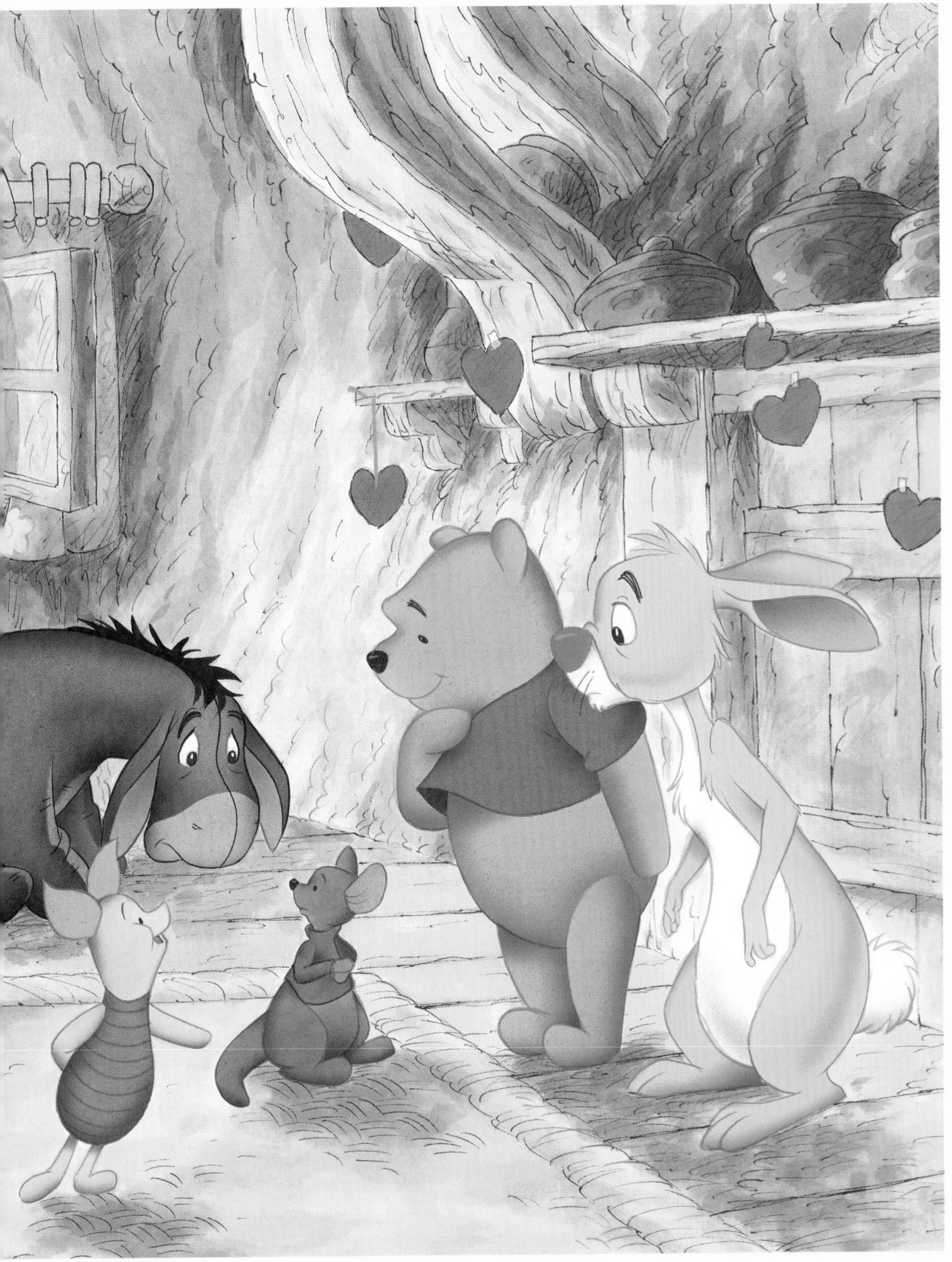

"And because 'I love you' are the most important words one person can say to another," sniffed Rabbit knowingly, "a valentine should say them in as many different ways as possible."

"What do you think, Eeyore?" Pooh asked the donkey, who was being even more silent than usual.

"Well, since you're askin'," rumbled Eeyore in his very slow way, "I suppose the sort of valentine you're plannin' is definitely one way of going about it."

"Then what're we waitin' for?" hooted Tigger. "Christmas?"

"I'll get my tools," said Gopher gleefully.

"I'll get my dictionary," said Rabbit.

"I'll clean up when we're through," said Piglet.

"And I'll tell you what I think of it when it's finished," announced Eeyore, "if anyone is interested, that is."

Considering the immensity of the undertaking that lay before them, Kanga's valentine took shape in a surprisingly short space of time.

Gopher chiseled a huge heart out of a boulder he had been saving for just such a special occasion. It was twice as tall as Tigger balanced on the very tip-top of his tail.

"Impressive," everyone told Gopher when he was done.

The irrepressible feline wasted not a moment painting the heart with the most spectacular colors he could think of, bright orange with black stripedy stripes. "Posilutely splendiferous," Tigger purred when he'd completed his task.

And as Piglet swept up the work area, Roo climbed up onto the obliging Eeyore's back and wrote "I love you" on the heart in his very best printing. Everyone agreed that although it was very small as printing goes, it couldn't have been more neatly done.

Then, after consulting a dictionary so thick he'd had to haul it all the way from his house in a wheelbarrow, Rabbit added a great many words and phrases, including "Kiss me good night" and "Do your homework" and "Eat your vegetables," as well as "Smoochface," "Pookums," and — Rabbit's personal favorite — "Snugglebunny." He assured the others that all these things said precisely the same thing Roo had printed, only in different ways.

The completed project was a magnificent, no, an *impressive*, sight. The friends were all quite pleased with themselves until Roo, after studying the valentine for some time, suddenly blurted out, "But how am I going to get this to my mother?"

Spirits plummeted. No one had thought of how this valentine was going to be delivered to Kanga. Mailing it was out of the question. Even if an envelope of the proper size could have been produced in time, the correct number of postage stamps would have weighed more than the valentine itself.

Sitting in a sad little circle, the friends were unable to come up with any helpful ideas at all.

"I guess we're finished," sighed Tigger hopelessly.

"Then now's the time I'll tell you what I thought," announced Eeyore, "if you really want to know, that is."

"Oh, I think we really do want to know, Eeyore," said Pooh.

"I think," said Eeyore even more ponderously than usual, "what I thought all along. This valentine is definitely *one* way of doing it."

"Why, Eeyore!" exclaimed Pooh. "I believe that's very helpful!"

"It is?" brayed the startled donkey.

"It is?" repeated the others in a single surprised voice.

"Certainly," explained Pooh, furrowing his brow. "If this is *one* way of doing a valentine, that means there must be a *two* way! *One* does not, after all, mean *only*. It means the something before the *next* thing...doesn't it?"

Everyone exchanged amazed smiles and nods as Roo leaped excitedly to his feet.

"You're right, Pooh! You're right!" he shouted. "And I know exactly what the next thing is, thanks to all of you!"

That evening at just about suppertime (according to the rumblings of Pooh's tummy), they all watched as Roo presented his mother, Kanga, with a handful of beautiful wildflowers.

"These flowers," Roo explained to Kanga, "say 'I love you'..."

Pooh poked Piglet to make sure he'd heard, but the smile on Piglet's face revealed that he hadn't missed a thing.

"...and," Roo continued, "they say it in very bright colors."

Tigger puffed out his chest so far he nearly fell off his tail.

"And because the flowers are all different kinds, they say 'I love you' in lots of different ways."

Rabbit remarked that he had something in his eye so no one should think he was crying or anything.

"And," said Roo, completing the presentation, "they're the most *impressive* valentine I could carry all by myself."

Gopher blew his nose into a brightly patterned bandanna.

"Thank you, Roo, dear," smiled Kanga. Sniffing the flowers, she added, "I couldn't have asked for a more perfect valentine."

As mother and son embraced, Tigger leaned over to Pooh and whispered, "But what'll we do with the valentine *we* made?"

"Keep it right where it is," Pooh whispered back. "It will remind us that there can be a lot of 'I love you' in every day if you know just where to look for it."